Bringing Big Emotions to a Bigger God

GOD, I feeL SCARED

written by
Michelle Nietert, LPC-S
Tama Fortner

illustrated by
Nomar Perez

To the One who brightens the darkness around me (Psalm 18:28).
—TF

To Tama, my co-author and now friend. I'm so glad you found that email in your spam folder. Words cannot express my gratitude enough to you and our Zonderkidz team. Without all of you, this series would still be a dream in my head instead of a tool for kids and counselors to use for years to come.
—MN

To God, for allowing me to use my talents and skills to bring this timely message to light and make a difference in the lives of those who have put their trust in Him.
—NP

ZONDERKIDZ

God, I Feel Scared
Copyright © 2023 by Michelle Nietert and Tama Fortner
Illustrations © 2023 by Michelle Nietert and Tama Fortner

Requests for information should be addressed to:
Zonderkidz, 3900 Sparks Drive, Grand Rapids, Michigan 49546

Hardcover ISBN 978-0-310-14089-4
Audio download ISBN 978-0-310-14091-7
Ebook ISBN 978-0-310-14090-0

Tama Fortner is represented by Cyle Young of Cyle Young Literary Elite, LLC. Michelle Nietert is represented by the literary agency of The Blythe Daniel Agency, Inc., P.O. Box 64197, Colorado Springs, CO 80962.

Zonderkidz is a trademark of Zondervan.

Zondervan titles may be purchased in bulk for educational, business, fundraising, or sales promotional use. For information, please email SpecialMarkets@Zondervan.com.

Zonderkidz is a trademark of Zondervan.

Illustrations: Nomar Perez
Editors: Katherine Jacobs/Jacque Alberta
Design and art direction: Cindy Davis

Printed in India

23 24 25 26 27 28 / REP / 21 20 19 18 17 16 15 14 13 12 11 10 9 8 7 6 5 4 3 2 1

When God made you, He gave you feelings.

Some emotions feel wonderful, like happy, excited, and surprised.
But others aren't as fun to feel, like mad, and sad, and …

scared.

Scared can show up as a worry, like wondering what will happen next. Or it can grow bigger, like shadows creeping across a dark room. Some scared can get really huge, like when lightning flashes and thunder kabooms!

Scared can sneak up when it's time to try something new—and you're afraid you won't get it right. Or it can jump out when someone yells, "Boo!"

You might feel scared when someone you love is hurt or sick. You're worried about them ... and maybe a little nervous it could happen to you too.

Scared sometimes happens when you feel all alone—like getting lost from your mom, when you can't find a friend, or when it's time to head off to school.

Scared isn't the most fun emotion to feel, but it can be God's gift to you. It's His way of sounding an alarm and letting you know something might be wrong.

Scared can show up in a tummy ache or a belly full of butterflies.

You might shiver and shake from head to toe.

Your cheeks could get hot, or your hands could feel cold.

Your shoulders might shrug up tight around your ears.

Scared could even slip out in tears ...

or burst out in anger!

Scared might make you feel frozen in place, like you can't move, or speak, or think! Your breathing may speed up, or it could feel like you can't breathe at all. You may think you're going to be sick!

You might stand up tall, ready to fight. Or you might want to run away and hide.

Scared looks different on each person's face. Some open their eyes extra big to see as much as they can. Others squeeze their eyes shut and wish the fear would go away.

You might clench your teeth together with your lips closed tight.
Or your mouth might pop open wide. And sometimes, your face
won't show any feelings at all.

Scared spills out in words like ...

You don't understand.

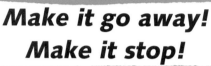

Make it go away!
Make it stop!

I want my mommy . . .
my daddy . . .
my best snuggly friend.

And sometimes, being scared
won't let any words come out at all.

It's okay to feel worried. And it's okay to feel scared—even when you're trying not to show it. Remember to tell yourself that you're going to be okay.

Some fears are big, and you'll need to ask for help. Talk to a grown-up. Talk to a friend—because talking can help you figure things out. Most of all, talk to God. He knows exactly how to protect and comfort you.

There are many kinds of fears that you can face, but you never have to face them alone. God is always there to help. He never leaves you all on your own.

When you're scared, what can you do to feel safe again? First, give your feeling a name. Say, "I feel worried" … or afraid … or frightened. Pick the word that best fits what you are feeling.

If you're too scared to think of a word, take a deep, slow breath—in through your nose and out through your mouth. Then take another … or two! Breathing will help you think again so you can find your words.

Next, look around you and pay attention. What's going on? Think about the thing that's scaring you. Ask yourself some questions, like ...

If I were feeling big and brave, how scary would this really be?

What could I do to make this fear smaller?

Could I worry about this for a minute and then move on and do something else?

Sometimes scared will pop up and then quickly disappear again, like turning on the light in a dark room. Other times, those feelings of fear try to stick around and hang out with you.

Push those scary thoughts away by putting other thoughts in your brain, like *God will help me fight this fear.*

Try watching a show, dancing to a song, or playing a favorite game. Draw a picture of your fears or write them down in a story. Then wad up that paper and … stomp them out!

You could also try doing the very thing you're afraid to do. Because when you face your fears—when you don't let them stop you—you're being *brave*.

With every fear you face, your brave gets bigger and stronger.
Then you can help others fight their fears too.

Scared happens to us all, and that's okay. But God doesn't want you to stay afraid. That's why He promises to stick right by your side. He's bigger and stronger than any fear you'll ever face.

God's love and protection are everywhere and all around you ... even when you're feeling scared.

God has not given us a spirit of fear, but of power and of love and of a sound mind.
—2 Timothy 1:7

Dear Parent,

It's important for children to experience all their feelings—even the hard ones. When you recognize that your child is feeling scared, encourage them to talk about and name their emotions. Let them know it's okay to feel this way. Give them opportunities to express and release those feelings—through tears, drawing, or writing. Do this even for the "ordinary" childhood fears. (Yes, including the ones that seem unimportant or even a little silly to you.) A child needs at least ninety seconds to recognize and process an emotion in order to release it—or it could cycle back even stronger.

There are some very real things we need to be afraid of in our world. Help your child learn the difference between truly dangerous things and fears they need to face. And teach them how to respond by trusting God with both kinds of fear.

There are times, though, when fear can be so huge and overwhelming that it paralyzes your child. Teach your child *calm-down skills* to help them calm their minds and bodies so that they can then face their fears. Calm-down skills include:

- Belly breathing, which begins by lying down with a book on your belly. Breathe in deeply through the nose and out through the mouth, with breaths deep enough to make the book move.
- Blow bubbles or blow on a pinwheel to make it spin really fast.
- Squeeze a stress ball.
- Watch the glitter in a glitter tube move up and down as the tube is turned.
- Practice *mindfulness* by finding five things you can see, four you can touch, three you can hear, two you can smell, and one you can taste.
- Think of a place where you feel completely safe and imagine yourself there.
- Repeat a favorite Bible verse or calming phrase. (Second Timothy 1:7 is a great one!)

If, after a few weeks of use, none of these skills are working, reach out to a doctor, school counselor, or mental health professional for guidance.

By helping your child learn to process and control their fears, you are gifting them with a skill they'll use their entire lives. For more information and ideas on helping children cope with emotions, please visit GodIFeel.com.